You Can't Go Back

John Hartzell

MILTON & HUGO L.L.C.
4407 Park Ave., Suite 5
Union City, NJ 07087, USA

Website: *www. miltonandhugo.com*
Hotline: *1- 888-778-0033*
Email: *info@miltonandhugo.com*

Ordering Information:
Quantity sales. Special discounts are granted to corporations, associations, and other organizations. For more information on these discounts, please reach out to the publisher using the contact information provided above.

Library of Congress Control Number:	2025910047	
ISBN-13:	979-8-89285-565-5	[Paperback Edition]
	979-8-89285-564-8	[Digital Edition]

Rev. date: 05/13/2025

Hello, my name is John R. Hartzell and just want to touch briefly with you about the purpose and meaning behind what your about to read and may experience.

This book was written in direct correlation to what I learned on my journey. This journey was on attempt to heal myself mentally and spiritually. This may not be a journey that actually ends once you start but this is a huge portion of it.

I never intended on writing down the results until a dear friend insisted that I had to write it. When I met this dear Friend "Adrien Ivring is his name" he was in a very bad and dark place mentally as I was when I decided to start my own journey, everything in this book I shared with him in an attempt to save his life. Once all the dust settled we both agreed this book needed to be written.

I then went on to spend an entire year of just writing, and I do believe it's time to share this book with everyone else. I told myself that all the work would be worth it if it could help at least 10 people. It's already helped 5 people so it's already half way there.

Please if anything in here inspires you please email and let me know which part if any at all. I hope if anything it just may help a little.

It's not a stimulation you're just hiding.

Drown the noise and put in the work.

You have to use your imagination, your spirit will thank you.

99.9% of people are afraid of their own imagination, why should you fear their opinion?

Don't ever sleep on nobody and make sure they only fear you for your hustle.

You can't wake up and think someone is going to come be you for you.

Do it without to any greed so once the results and votes come in they'll be sustainable.

Only thing to fear from a man's perspective is to no longer be in control of your own life.

Wisdom is extremely complex, you can speak it all you want but unless you know the energy it carries it won't mean nothing.

It's a journey for sure. It's a process, the man or person you are in the beginning will change for better or for worse.

You got to realize you're the one putting one foot in front of the other.

"You are the Center of your Own bullshit"

"Julie Medves"

So take it slow as slow as you can handle, observe, focus, learn, write, teach, smell, laugh, cry, fight, yell, love, Imagine, even appreciate.

The world has so much to offer. Billions of people and nature has existed threw an amount of time we could truly never understand.

Everything in life is just nearly a distraction from the fact that we just live and die, so make sure you're distracted with what you love.

I left high school as soon as I realized it was just a popularity contest. 10th grade, 2nd week.

I'll never be part of their social experiment you want motivation go a week with no food you'll be hungrier than ever.

Constantly treating my body like a vessel.

You'll be seen as a King/Queen when the success speaks, for its self.

Our answers we so desperately urn for are right behind our excuses.

I take pride in what I do its okay if you don't I don't judge no body.

"you can't judge me shit I'm of an angel."

No disrespect but I got enough trauma "(I don't need to hear yours.)" emotions keep you in bed your mind gets you out of it.

On my grind baby

A beautiful mind equals a beautiful life

A beautiful mind is all that is needed to have a beautiful LIFE.

Right or wrong isn't just the questioning of good or bad it's also whether or not its love or hate. Sometimes people be forgetting your on a team.

The worlds meant to be beautiful not angry.

Learn to leave your emotions at the clock in/out machine.

Sometimes you'll forget were a team. The people around you the people in your circle, them newly strangers ya that's your team.

If there questioning everything you do, it's because you're on their radar.

The only thing that positivity changes your presence and relevance is your actions.

Nothing truly needs spoke on. Put your phone back on the wall where it's meant to be.

You allowed them to drain you!

Accountability is so important. You have to stop pretending appreciation and accountability are difficult.

You're going to have to wait 10, 15, 20 years to be worth something as a man. Eventually they'll be bringing up who you use to be. Just keep grinding they can't tear it apart if it was built without greed.

What's the difference between a moment and a memory?

If you would of been the man you are today, yesterday it wouldn't of made sense.

The slower you say it the more it means.

It's actually less scary if you look up.

Only way to truly fail is to not make any more attempts.

The days you don't feel good are the days you have to put in the most work.

That shit you're feeding yourself is poisons to your imagination make better health choices.

Stay humble, stay grateful, stay believing

You are not meant to do this alone. There's a reason why were all different it's what makes us so great at teamwork.

We're all just in some form or another a different shape. So it's easy to argue that were all perfectly imperfect so be mindful of the way you speak to yourself. It will consitily change your results in life.

Teamwork makes the dream work is a saying as old as time. The people around you for better or worse is your team.

Doesn't matter how much you don't like your brother or some random stranger that's your team, and what you do with it is on you.

It doesn't matter what you believe in, you cannot move in negative directions and end up somewhere positive. You need to believe in something.

They are going to be constantly expecting you to be them and you have to forever choose to be you.

Every single day is a choice. Which you have to make every time you wake up now you can choose to sit around until its bed time again and again.

Whether you want to accept it or not staying still is a negative movement if it could have been a positive movement and instead you choose negative without even realizing it you moved your life in a negative direction.

The blame game only gets you so far. You can blame your parents for the first ten years shit maybe even the first twenty but who you gonna blame for the 3rd decade?

Once you can see your blaming everything around you for your trash perspective you run otta shit to blame real quick.

Don't sit around waiting for someone to come guide you out the dark because they may never come.

Choosing to not think about it is simply you just accepting it's easier to not take any action to change it or fix it.

Be honest,

It is okay to be Human.

Maybe it's all just simply less work?

I will never allow myself to love someone/something I'm not allowed to.

Happiest when I'm grinding!

Enjoy yourself today!!!

It's all just a popularity contest anyway.

How many people can you get to talk about you for the right reasons?

No amount of peace will allow you to get comfortable if you grew threw the struggle.

Think for yourself don't allow

Others to think for you.

How you treat yourself is a statement on how you will allow others to treat you.

If you have fallen get up!

I stopped trying to control my life and just focused on me. Controlling 100% of your life is impossible.

Nature will forever play its own part in your life.

What is it that you know about life that can prove or explain to me why a simple creature such as a ant can't have a soul?

There's always more than meets the eye

I'll never allow anyone! To turn my passion off ever! Again!!

And either should you!

I told myself to stop working and my ass just kept on working

It's hated until everybody doing it. Be yourself.

Spend your time providing life will provide for you.

Nature.

Appreciate nature!

Steady letting the success speak for its self.

Once my kids were grown I knew it was time for me to go after what's mine.

Most important question I've ever asked my self___

What I'm I doing wrong?

Sooo..

Too much belief in things you don't even know are certain?

Figuring out why to you is what makes it a process.

Every man needs an office a space to think and process thoughts.

Have trust even when all is lost.

What's earned is yours for the keeping.

There's people winning and they built with the same shit you are!

Science This is

Being all business will have people looking at you differently.

Being able to show your ability makes you stronger, as does your ability to show vulnerability

I'm stronger than I believe god please answer my prayers.

Everyone pretends to be so respectful when kids are around but around just adults no one cares seems to care how they affect people.

Age can never defend if you're a human? Why does someone's age change how you act?

Use your words!

It all about the money when they are handling you but once you begin matching that energy its hold on wait a minute, be patience

If it was all business when they was handling you but now they wanna change the tempo.

Once you match this energy they'll throw you aside

Am I to be completely self-made?

Forget it I'll never let a another soul turn off my passion ("not even" "my own")

I've never showed off you just lack action, easier to spend time hating on others than to work on yourself. Stop constantly producing negative energy.

I'll never participate.

I simply play the game by not playing the game.

Focus on the positive. Just simply means focus on what's ahead.

Only way to change the repetition in life is within the way you interact with the people around you.

Your mind is going to try to get you to hate, it may seem like it's the easier route in the moments. Stay away from it!

Don't get caught up in nobody's popularity contest. Just be the best version of yourself possible.

In the end happiness is created and chose.

Limit nothing but their access to you. They'll stay expecting you to be them, you must stay choosing to be you.

Your soul isn't and can't be the place for their hate. You have to stop storeing their pain.

Happiness is a choice. This isn't something you just acquire over time from achieving goals, breaking limits, or love even at its highest form to exist to today's standards. You can achieve love at its purest form, yet still wake up and decide to be unhappy about a certain moment and in general as well. Say you finally wake up and one morning check in your account to find 200,000 dollars, even though this maybe the most you've ever had, you could run right threw the money. Even a random day as a rich person you can become more miserable than the worse days you've come to experience.

I know what I'm simply saying is happiness is literally a choice. It's a nonstop never ending question "am I ever going to be happy?" the truth is yes every time you choose to be happy you will feel happiness. Every time you choose sadness you're going to feel it and be it.

Look not everyone is going to be capable of choosing happiness for 24 hours a day 7 days a week. No one has that amount of ability with their energy. But like all energy you can build, grow and learn how to handle longer periods of happiness.

You start by spending 30 min to an hour a day choosing to be happy and building it into longer periods of time that your capable of choosing your own will to allow your soul to prosper.

But focus on setting aside time to your self for your self. This could be a million things. I'm sure there's something a little dangerous in your life that gives you what's called adrenaline and fear and nearly every other emotion at once. This is where you'll want to spend your peaceful, solitude moments. Doing so will give you an advantage to the disciple needed to build this strength.

That being said there's a lot of things you can add to your every day life to make that choice to be happy a lot easier and maybe even enjoyable. Lets say you met the beautiful girl of your dreams and feel invincible, which was a choice by the way. Say you wake up the next day and stump your toe and choose to allow anger to be your lead emotion. Now this is far fetched but not impossible. Let's say you continue to choose anger for your choices today. Then allowing yourself to bring in some confrontation with the love of your life and this causes her to lose a tiny bit of respect for you. This continues on until your constant choice of anger, maybe until it destroys you, then even end your relationship all together.

You may believe the world is against you or out to get you. The reality is that you choose this future by allowing anger to lead. Now you didn't mean for any of this to be your present But it is nearly because your unaware that there is a simple consit choice to be happy that's needed to stay happy.

This is needed to be done with every turn, choice, person, Job, significant other, and literally every moment your expecting happiness to exist on its own. You never will wake up and just randomly be happy without making the choice to be happy.

The idea that you should be doing this alone is just insane.

There are people in this world that are worth more value than the dollar bill, and on the other end everybody has the ability to be.

Your presence can stand for wealth.

I miss the days that I operated outta Love not Logic.

Hold your value in your mindset.

I'll tell you what looks good is a determined mother fucker taken care of themselves.

Hold your own accountability for personal value within your mindset.

Were subjected to nature, there's no getting past it

I'd never expect the best from anyone else if I didn't start with myself. We don't have the rights to no ones emotions, soul, or timeline. We just Don't.

You know that feeling when you've experienced one of them "that wet my wissle" moments and you fight to return to it again that's how you got to feel about being successful. You need that kind of hunger for it.

If you haven't mapped out what success looks like for you start there.

The main goal should be to inspire the results are so you know its working.

Spread Inspiration

Pray for good results.

Its easy to pick the life you have when you deny the life you want exist.

If you haven't started taking your life serious when??? Will you?

Stress is just time off your life. Stay away from it. Let the things giving it to you, keep it. Tell umm your keeping your time.

You gotta start jumping in the fire to prove to your self you can handle the heat.

Its easier if your not pretending beyond harder if you spend too much time pretending.

You only need one thing to live a beautiful life…

. . . . . .and that's a beautiful mind

When you truly come from a place of violence and high intensity you tend to not ask for more than just simple peace.

Protect your karma what you put into this world is what you get out of it.

It's never your fault for not understanding how to Love, you'll learn.

It's not difficult to be a good person and it's what makes your soul beautiful!

The reward for being a good person is a beautiful soul.

You have to figure out what makes you special.

What the fuck are you looking for? You're capable of more than you know.

No one truly give any thought toward your issues. You got to figure that shit out on your own. Everybody has their own problems. Judgement is different than animosity.

You will thrive better on a team or in a tribe. Never be afraid to express your love.

You have to be grateful for every dollar, nature proves to you.

College is mostly keeping the rich rich. There's literally amazing chefs all over the world that just started a restaurant and started cooking, And legit just failed enough times to succeed.

I challenge you to just write down one thing, one thing! That you want outta life this year.

Just write it down and throw it in the dresses draw and walk away. Forget about it.

Go right back to solving your problems alone because that I'll work

If you miss somebody and you don't do shit about it that's on you.

You have to protect your spirit. You gotta do it or else your pride is going to kill you.

You pride your ego it's all the same shit. Carrying your Pride and ego just basically means you got a closed mind.

Step 1 needs to be the removing of the hold your ego has on you. you'll need to start admitting you can't win on your own!!

There's positive sides of life, Your just here to find them

Aggression, be careful with it.

Judgement is what creates negativity

There is a lot of people that don't play the game with a decent set of morals some may not carry any at all.

Some may not even be aware of where theirs came from. Be careful who you allow to alter your opinion on things. Not everyone has good intentions for you or any at all.

The pain you trying to carry for everyone else, don't do that, its not your job. Now learning to carry another person's pain will teach you a lot, but its extremely difficult to do properly.

Move in positive directions you don't have to be a positive person nor a happy one to move in a positive direction

We can wake up everyday in a shit mood and still take our child to school on time, ending with maybe the child becoming successful and yield in our life moving in a positive direction.

Step 2: attach your self-worth to your intent.

Step 3: accept that emotional pain is real just don't be a loser about it.

There's an old saying,

> You got two ears and one mouth so listen twice as much as you speak.
>
> This just means to learn twice as much as you act.

You can have whatever you want out of this world just have to be humble and respectful and move with honor.

Side note, push ups will keep you alive

If you want to be able to take care of the people around you or in your circle your gonna have to put some work in.

The Better at connecting you get the closer you get to your circle, your people.

Parent hood is the most important job we have has humans. From a male and female perspective. Both equally as important this isn't an area of life your going to want to fail on as a result of the lack of presence or attempts.

The only way to truly fail is to never make anymore attempts, you're going to get things wrong.

Making mistakes will become a hobby but don't make them on purpose you won't learn as much from these ones, you'll learn more from the mistakes you don't see coming.

Not every move you make is going to be understood by everyone, you can only hope it may.

You get one run out of this race we call life, if we considered your life to be a marathon how would you run it?

I'd suggest you do it as slow and controlled as you possibly can. Don't get ahead of your self. Don't compete with the people around you in un healthy ways.

You'd truly be amazed by how far you can get simply by living as if your part of a team.

Easiest way to make a difference is just being a part of it you'll find where you fit in over time.

Luckily for us we do have control over a few things in life, one being the pace our lives move. Progress is totally up to us.

Especially once you begin to really get some control of the things in your life, the more pieces of the game you activate, the easier it is to play.

Your Imagination is and always will be your biggest and strongest weapon you have in this world! Don't ever lose it. Don't ever stop using it and always be mindful of what you feed it.

Believe me when I say being respectful is your second strongest weapon you have.

Your brother/sister is your third

Nothing produced externally can fix you within, the day you start the adventure it will create an ever lasting journey. The process of taking care of yourself, managing your self, expressing yourself, with all these different things you'll start developing the ability to have control within the life around you.

Start digging deep by taking accountability for the negative occurrences in your life.

Life is meant to be a process. Embrace the fact that you have weakness and strengths just like everyone else does, just because the weakness can't be seen doesn't mean it don't exist. Everybody has them.

Nobody's perfect. Live in your own truth. You got to be someone that's willing to spend some time getting things done.

At the beginning and end of every day all you really got is yourself. That's a different type of fight.

Whether you want to accept it or not, there is someone past present or future that will look to you for guidance.

So try to get somewhere healthy, somewhere worth leading to. Healthy doesn't mean complex. Simple will work.

Happiness is a choice, not a reaction. You have got to start the process of mastering the act of not caring how others feel about you.

The cool part of being the only person with access to your language is you can create it. Be mindful how you speak to your self it matters, speak honestly.

The only difference between you and anybody else is their ability to believe in themselves. Never fear accountability. The presence you carry matters.

No matter how bad the storms can get, never stop smiling with your heart. The more time you spend living in the past, the less time you spend in the present.

Face your past, heal threw it, that way you'll get more time in the present, and more peace as well.

Nature is constantly reminding us that growth is the point. Don't ignore that and always leave room for it.

The way you treat yourself will act as a guide for others to treat you.

Growing up without the presence of my father actually gave me compete control over the man I became. Don't go thinking I'm saying it was cool to grow up without a father because it wasn't. I'm simply saying I didn't let it become an excuse for my failures and mistakes.

Don't get caught up in blaming others or allowing your excuses to hold you back.

Don't ever let anyone convince you that this isn't a eat or be eaten world because it is.

Write stuff down. Things like why your fighting, believing, and not giving up. So when you do tend to lose a little faith you have a little something to resort back to.

Do not stop looking for reasons to live they exist in abundance. You'll never know when you may need a new one. This isn't an area in life you will want to get caught with your pants down.

Power comes from the things we cannot see. So Don't go chasing power, odds are is you'll get it once you can truly handle it. Once you begin to attract power you'll receive it at levels you can manage it. Therefore allowing you to maintain it effectively.

You're going to wake up one day and realize that life is literally just waking up and going threw the same motions over and over again. So in order to live any kinda significe life you're going to have to learn to alter these days.

The best way to alter your life is to say hi to a stranger.

Your pride your ego none of that really exist, let them go. Stop trying to be something and just be someone.

I know it may sound crazy, but you need some kind of edge in order to survive this thing we call life. Being normal will never get the job done.

One of the biggest things I've noticed is that it really bothers someone to hear somebody's dream.

Do not ever fear your own Imagination, it is showing you things you are meant to see. It is incredible, its a powerful force, you must use it.

I carry myself with respect. And this simply means I do not move in negative directions. Doesn't matter who you are, the deeper you dig yourself into a hole the longer it takes to get out of.

If you try to give power to a humbled, peaceful man he'd probably won't want anything to do with it. He Might Just tell you to keep it.

Once you get/have some power. Don't give it away to greed!

You wouldn't believe how many people around you, simply do not want to live, yet expected to contribute.

Which yes is necessary. But if you're looking for a reason to fight to live. Understand that it's the fight it's self that makes it worth the fight. Stop focusing so much on to why, and just fight. You'll find a reason(s) for it later, they will come.

If your ever wondering if it's worth the fight. Yes it is, there's more to life than you can normally see in dark places. Trust life to be a process, it will forever be one.

If the world does truly bless you with a want you have be grateful. Blessings are as rare, as the people that create them.

Life gets extremely simple once you start learning how to believe, just do it. What do you have to lose? Just for one second believe the future will be better.

You only need to improve 1% a day to truly make an impact. 1% a day for a third of your year is like 120 days or so, that's an 120% improvement on your life over only one year.

Don't go pissing in nobody's cornflakes for the other half of the year, thinking the scale is going to weight in your favor. It never will, winning is a possibility, but the game isn't setup for you to win.

Every level you achieve is set up to send you back to the level you just came from, learning what level you want to survive on, that's peace.

Power and greed is why peace is so rare, your existence was meant to be peaceful any defenses toward it is not being truthful.

you're here for a reason, your special live in

your truth you're a blessing to the world.

I've learned to stop talking to people that wasn't listening.

People are going to teach you your gifts by using you for them.......!

Life is beautiful when you learn to see it for what it is. Which is a process.

If it was your grandmas purpose to be the butter for your family, who holds the torch? Somebody has to step up!

Everyone wants a family no one wants to sacrifice anything for it thou.

Greed is pointless

Expressing your self will always require courage.

Money only brings what the greed behind it brings.

Be easy on yourself

They'll continue trying to trick you into using hate.

Greed is never the answer

If you can't start your day with you! Don't start it go back to bed, try again later.

You don't make decisions for a place you've never been.

You take steps.

Nothings that deep but be mindful who you share with.

Hustle til they swallow their pride and say thank you

Everyone puts their pants on the same way in the morning

Create your your memories and intentions with your heart.

Fight against it, it will feel heavy

Roll with it, it will feel light.

What do you think was going to happen when you take all that energy your putting into everyone else and invested it in yourself?

You can measure character by how they use their heart.

You Can't claim the glory for being great if you can't accept responsibly for when you're not.

I wanted more out of Me

Were constantly saying we want things outta life but the wants don't start with "life" they start with I.

I want a new house

I want a new Harley

I want my kids to thrive

I want my family/friends healthily

So get after it, but it starts with You.

They truly Judge you

Based on your results

And nothing else

Every time in your day to day life you overcome shit. You are the shit, and you know it. – you know who you are – just because you haven't learn to play the game doesn't mean you deserve to be treated like a slave.

Everybody is so worried about what everyone else is being, that they just become them.

They can only control your time that keeps you from the things you love never can they control your ability.

If you can't teach what you've learned then learning it was pointless.

Be kind to your self everyday! Its not selfish.

You can move to a time zone that accommodates "your" "morning".

You're your ticket out!

Be better by changing yourself, you get better by allowing yourself to grow

Go on a journey in your mind with yourself.

You can literally say hi to the whole world at once now.

Running a business is not that complicated of a process, its how you build it not what you build that matters. When you got twenty different people telling you your gift don't ignore it.

Laughter keeps you healthy.

Use new energy everyday.

Are you focusing on everything that doesn't make a difference?

What's it going take for you to accept something. There's nothing wrong with wanting time to yourself. No one has figured it out yet.

Are you allowing yourself to grow?

How you do one thing

Is how you do everything?

You do you

I'll do me

I'll find the blessing

Behind the pain!

And I'll handle my

thoughts process

thanks thou

everything in life is a

distraction.

What part of the movie do you enjoy the most beginning?
Middle? End?

. . . or other

There's no job

   No career

   No Break-threw

   No relationship

That's going to be your ticket to happiness

      You are your

      Ticket to happiness!

We're more complicated than you think.

   You have to start with You!

   Not your dad or your mom or money. You have to start
with yourself! If you have kids already and you haven't went
on your Journey even your kids have to give you time to
grow and start *With yourself.*

When happiness comes do you allow it? What do you do with happiness when it does come? Does it come? Will it come?

What part of the story do you shine? What part do you enjoy?

If you truly care about others, you will be ok with not being the greatest.

The more time you spend thinking of the future the less time you spend in the present. We got to start taking care of each other or the worlds never going to get/be better if we don't.

You grow differently when you are loved properly

You're going to continue to ask the question til you answer it.

They'll hate you for caring until you stop. Then hate you for not caring.

Artist:

　Just a title you gain

Once you've learned how to express your creativity.

There are two things that truly matter

　　　　People &

　　　　Nature

I pay attention to people when there having a bad day, who they are then is who they are truly.

　When your spirit is healthy you're going to walk differently.

　Skin color never has and never will define a person's soul.

　Talking about murder and robbery being bad/illegal but no one ever speaks on breaking someone's soul.

Difficult

If

You

Choose

www.ingramcontent.com/pod-product-compliance
Lightning Source LLC
Chambersburg PA
CBHW022347040426
42449CB00006B/752